I0025867

Solved!

Unsolvable immigration problems are solved right here.

We did our part in bringing all of the domestic solutions for illegal residents to you in their full versions and now again in this sampling of the Whitman's Sampler / CliffsNotes-like versions. In each of the three chapters of this mini sampler, you'll find a book purpose section followed by an introduction, followed by a Preface and a few chapters. To differentiate chapters of sampler book from the about books, we use a Ch designator rather than Chapter, followed by the Chapter number. That's all we need right here for an intro. Here are the titles of the three immigration books that are part of the Top Ten American Political Books for 2018. Enjoy! The books in this mini sampler are highlighted below in bold.

1. Taxation Without Representation Fourth Edition-- Can the U.S. avoid another "Boston Tea Party?"
2. DELETE the EPA! EPA agenda is not to save human lives. Is its insidious goal world population control?
3. Deport All Millennials Now! It ought to be easy. They'll line up like it's a free vacation
4. No Free Lunch—Pay Back Welfare The first book that recommends that welfare should not be free money
5. Wipe Out All Student Debt Now! Unique solutions to the $1.45 Trillion debt accumulation
6. Boost Social Security Now! A solution to get Seniors out of the poorhouse; Hey buddy, can you spare a dime?
7. **Legalizing Illegal Aliens Via Resident Visas A great Americans-first plan which saves $trillions. Learn how!**
8. **Pay-To-Go--An America-first immigration fix. No more deportations, except for bad guys**
9. Obamacare: A One-Line Repeal Congress must get this done.
10. **60 Million Illegals in America!!! A simple, America-first solution!**

BRIAN W. KELLY

LETS GO ! PUBLISH

Copyright 2018 Brian W. Kelly
Title *Solved*
Subtitle: *Unsolvable immigration problems are solved right here*
Editor   Brian P. Kelly
Author   Brian W. Kelly

Published by: LETS GO PUBLISH!
Publisher: Brian P. Kelly   brian@brianpkelly.com
Editor: Brian P. Kelly
P.O Box 621   Wilkes-Barre, PA   www.letsgopublish.com

Library of Congress Copyright Information Pending
Book Cover Design by B. W. Kelly;
Editing and original writing by B. P. Kelly

ISBN Information: The International Standard Book Number (ISBN) is a unique machine-readable identification number, which marks any book unmistakably. The ISBN is the clear standard in the book industry. 159 countries and territories are officially ISBN members. The Official ISBN for this book is also on the outside cover: **978-1-947402-33-1** ---

---

The price for this work is: **$7.95 USD**

10   9   8   7   6   5   4   3   2   1

Release Date: February 2018

Executive Summary:

This book has a unique structure. It consists of three chapters taken from a book titled, Top Ten American Political Books for 2018. The three chapters are synopses of three books I wrote as a total solution for the problem of 60 million illegal aliens residing in the USA.

- 60 Million Illegal Aliens in America!!!
- Pay-to-Go
- Legalizing Illegal Aliens Via Resident Visas

The original full book titles shown above were written in the fall of 2017. The key immigration programs for the 60 million resident interlopers are called Pay to Go and Resident Visa.

These programs solve the problem with 60 million interlopers residing in the US, and also solve DACA and Sanctuary Cities. They also set the stage for better management of current green card holders and anchor citizens.

Here is the solved problem in a nutshell. The benefits come to Americans through a decrease in the crime rate and not having to pay the cost of welfare for non-Americans enrolled in the Resident Visa Program.

1. Crimes:

The 2011 GAO report titled CRIMINAL ALIEN STATISTICS shows the extent of the crime problem caused by illegal aliens. The situation has gotten worse, not better. The report examined 251,000 criminal aliens in federal, state, and local prisons and jails. Those aliens were arrested nearly 1.7 million times for close to three million criminal offenses.

Sixty-eight percent of those in federal prison and 66 percent of those in state prisons were from Mexico. Their offenses ranged from homicide and kidnapping to drugs, burglary, and larceny. The real numbers are actually worse as the statistics are admittedly lacking those crimes committed by illegal aliens who are not incarcerated. The numbers would be higher because prosecutors often agree to drop criminal charges against an illegal alien when they are assured that ICE will deport the alien. We can estimate the cost of illegal aliens on the us criminal system as follows

- At Approximately $300 per arrest, 1.7 million arrests = $510 million
- At approximately $60.00 per jail day, 365 jail days per year for 251,000 criminal aliens comes to $5.5 billion
- At approximately $700 as an estimate of the cost of a crime, with 3 million crimes committed by illegal aliens, this comes to this comes to 2.1 billion.
- The total cost of illegal lien crime is thus $8.1 billion, which is more than likely a low estimate.

2. Dollar costs for medical, welfare, etc.

An estimated 49 percent of households headed by legal immigrants used one or more welfare programs in 2012, compared to 30 percent of households headed by natives. Less-educated legal immigrants make extensive use of every type of welfare program, including cash, food, Medicaid, and housing. Recent restrictions on new legal immigrants' access to welfare have not worked. They have not prevented them from accessing programs at high rates. The overwhelming majority of illegal immigrants have low levels of education; therefore, the high use of welfare associated with less-educated legal immigrants indicates that their legalization (green card) would likely increase welfare costs, particularly for cash and housing programs.

U.S. law enforcement agencies have observed that identity theft and illegal immigration "go hand in hand." Identity theft in many states is a felony. Because it is virtually impossible to live and work and collect benefits in the United States without documents, interlopers turn to fraudulent document dealers for falsified Social Security cards, forged drivers' licenses, counterfeit green cards, and a wide range of other phony documents. They commit identity theft to get what they need from the US system.

President Trump says that illegal aliens cost the US $113 billion per year. I have statistics that show that this number is as high as $500 billion per year. Moreover, professional analysis of the reduced and lost wages for Americans considering that illegal aliens often work for below minimum wages creates a net loss to Americans approaching another $500 Billion per year. If Americans knew the cost, they surely would not opt to pay for foreigners.

Think of what can be done with as much as $500 billion in treasury savings and by increasing the purchasing power of Americans by $500 billion.

The consensus cost for welfare for non-citizens is about $30,000 per person per year. It is staggering. Americans would choose not to afford it. Many legal and illegal aliens use welfare as a means of survival.

SOLVED: The Pay-To-Go and Resident Visa Programs solves the problem 100%

These two programs are paid for by either illegal interlopers on welfare agreeing to voluntary deportation with a $20,000 stipend, or agreeing to the terms of the new "no American cost" Resident Visa" program. The stipulations include full vetting, jobs for Americans first, never voting, no citizenship, and no freebies of any kind. Those not approved for the resident visa program may use self-deportation with a nice stipend through Pay-to-Go or coerced deportation.

As noted, each welfare recipient costs as much as $30,000 per year. The backup dollar figures are in the chapter synopses in this book, and in the detailed books.

At 100% participation, which would be a requirement for illegals already in the country, estimates are as high as $500 billion per year cost savings. Plus, with the negative impact on lower wages, and loss of jobs negated with these programs, another $500 Billion of additional citizen purchasing power would be expected. These are huge numbers and they are real. The US can be as much as $1Trillion to the good. If we can figure a way for countries to take back their criminals, there is another $8.1 billion to be recovered.

The cost savings come when all foreign interlopers have either self-deported, been deported by coercion, or have signed up for the Resident Visa Program. To repeat, once these two programs are in effect, illegal aliens who have not signed up for either of these very generous programs will be deported.

Those currently on welfare may apply for a two-year non-renewable welfare extension to get them through the transition period. At the end of the two years, there will be no more welfare for Resident Visa Holders. Those in this status may be granted benefits under the Pay-to-Go program including the $20,000 stipend.

An accountability system should be built anticipating the savings of the programs. During the vetting process, demographic and financial information must be collected on each interloper. This information should not be discarded lost. Instead it should be stored in a permanent accountability database which may be used to store any temporary welfare and/or medical charges for later repayment.

There would be no charge at all for an interloper choosing the Pay-to-Go option and all transportation costs to wherever, would be covered. After one year at $30,000 off the system, this money will all be back in the treasury.

To attain a resident visa, the first-year fee would be $200 and the annual renewal fee would be $100.00. Electronic vetting would be used to determine the annual renewals for the Resident Visa. Resident Visa holders will lose their approved status by not abiding by the stipulations of their contract or by committing a crime. Before being granted status, the interlopers must agree to all the terms and be vetted first at a cursory level and then in person. T

No more fake ID's, no identity theft, no DACA, no welfare. No voting, no citizenship. What is there for Americans, Democrat or Republican, not to like , Those approved get resident visas. There would be no need for Sanctuary Cities because there would be no illegals in the country ever again. DACA children will be given 10-year free Resident Visas as a compromise.

Isn't this what everybody wants? There are more details in synopses chapters in this book as well as and in the detailed books

Thank you,

Brian W. Kelly
Author

Preface:

Brian W. Kelly immensely enjoyed putting this mini summary book together. Being the author of each of the ten underlying books, which outline the major solutions for the severe domestic ills afflicting America today, made it easy for Brian to pick and choose the synopses that would serve as a Whitman's Sampler / CliffsNotes version that addresses illegal immigration. More specifically these three books solve the problem of having 60 million illegal residents in the US today. They do not focus on other issues such as the Wall, chain migration, etc.

Brian's objective was to put in one very condensed book the many solutions that have evaded the best of the best in Congress and the presidency for many years for one reason or another. Brian believes he did the job for Congress if we can get them to read this book. A secondary objective for Kelly was that he hoped that when any of the "CliffsNotes" versions were read, the reader would believe they had gotten the full picture of both the problem and the solution, even though the Whitman's Sampler synopsis would not contain all of the supporting detail.

Kelly is very happy that he was able to achieve both objectives with this Immigration Whitman's Sampler.

Why did Brian W. Kelly create this summary book?

After writing 147 published books, 145 non-fiction, and many published essays, Kelly learned that for some, seeing the answer before understanding the question, is another way to learn about a phenomenon. It may not be the best way but it sure is the easiest way to begin.

The US got into a pickle with immigration in 1986 with President Reagan's amnesty. Reagan was trying to be better than the resources that our country's collection of citizens could offer. People across the world saw the generosity of the US through its government and came here in droves afterwards, uninvited. That's why Kelly refers to them as interlopers (univited guests). Many worked hard but more and more came to not work and to take benefits from the American people and they chose gave nothing back. Americans cannot afford such people.

The same American politicians began to use those coming from poor conditions or s-holes as recently referred by President Trump, as pawns either to bring cheap labor to their donors or to do their best to vote Democrat in US National Elections. The situation is not pretty as politicians gave up their integrity to serve as loyal liberal progressive Democrats.

Brian loves America and like President Trump, he wants America to be great because great Americans, who are permitted to live without government constraints, are the vehicle which will make America and all Americans great again.

You will love this book because the immigration problem we face with 60 million interlopers living in the shadows, stealing milk and bread to survive, is solved right here. Look no further. Just open up your mind. We just have to get accustomed to a solution that does not deport the world of illegals who have come here for their own goodness. The vetting process in this program will separate the wheat from the chaff, and we will deport the chaff either with a $20,000 stipend or without if they give ICE a hard time.

Thank you for being so nice as to purchase this book and for helping keep America as the only place in the living world where freedom matters more than anything else.

I wish you the best.

Brian P. Kelly, Publisher
Wilkes-Barre, Pennsylvania

Table of Contents:

About the Author

Brian W. Kelly retired as an Assistant Professor in the Business Information Technology (BIT) program at Marywood University, where he also served as the IBM i and Midrange Systems Technical Advisor to the IT Faculty. Kelly designed, developed, and taught many college and professional courses. He continues as a contributing technical editor to a number of IT industry magazines, including "The Four Hundred" and "Four Hundred Guru," published by IT Jungle.

Kelly is a former IBM Senior Systems Engineer and IBM Mid Atlantic Area Specialist. His specialty was designing applications for customers as well as implementing advanced IBM operating systems and software facilities on their machines.

He has an active information technology consultancy. He is the author of 147 books and numerous technical articles. Kelly has been a frequent speaker at COMMON, IBM conferences, and other technical conferences.

Brian was a candidate for US Congress from Pennsylvania in 2010 and he brings a lot of experience to his writing endeavors. Brian Kelly knows how to solve most of the domestic problems in the US. Let's hope the Congress hears him out.

Chapter 1 Great Domestic Solutions Ready for 2018

The chapter was written by Brian Patrick Kelly, the author's oldest son, to help kickoff the book from which this book was extracted. It's title is Top 10 American Political Books for 2018. The covers of all ten books are shown in the montage below. Look in the second row for the immigration books.

Writing books can be fun

Prolific author Brian Kelly produces so many books in a given year that even his family cannot explain how he does it. His most popular books throughout the years, such as Great Moments in Alabama Football, have focused primarily on sports themes, but that is not his original claim to fame. Kelly's initial prior experience was problem solving in information technology and later political diagnosis and remedies. His U.S. domestic policy recommendations are second to none.

Anyone in the patriotic or conservative world who finds themselves flirting with finding an innovative solution to the domestic ills that have been eluding supposed experts for far too long will find their needs more than satisfied by one of Kelly's refreshing works. For open minded liberals or progressives, many of his answers can be hung on either side of the aisle.

Kelly's solutions are deceptively simple and occasionally counterintuitive at first glance. One's first question may be, "Can something so simple actually solve the problem?" After reading further and understanding his proposals, Kelly aspires to allow a new world of thought to unfold before the eyes and instill the positive belief that many of the nation's seemingly intractable maladies are indeed curable.

Historically, great thinkers and influential problem solvers possess an uncanny ability to translate otherwise arduous complex notions into language that any audience can readily understand. Kelly prides himself on cutting through argument, debate and doubt, and offers solutions that all can process and appreciate. Brian's plain talk solutions are authentic, cogent, clear, and palpable, quite unlike rocket science. He reveals a logical path for readers that culminate in "Of course!" rather than "What?!"

Brian has been quietly solving domestic problems for many years with various iterations of books that in 2017 have all been fine-tuned to meet the needs of today. Even his early books, such as No Taxation Without Representation, were considered groundbreaking. The 2017 editions of all of Kelly's books written to solve America's most urgent domestic issues are his most refined yet.

His readers are continually amazed that a layman who spent his life as a technician for IBM could redeploy his analytical and problem-solving skills to the broader challenges facing America. He has accomplished this repeatedly and in 2017, he has done it again by preparing the fixes that the Congress and the President can deploy in 2018.

With this book of synopses, Brian Kelly now has one hundred and forty-six books to his credit. They vividly describe various aspects of American life. A good many of Kelly's 2017 books specify how the nation can address its many challenges in the current century.

While Kelly may allocate personal time to offering advice on issues like how many crossing guards are needed at a local intersection in Wilkes-Barre, Pennsylvania, he does not purport to be an expert on such matters which he has not yet studied in depth. By contrast, Kelly has spent years contemplating the major social and domestic problems in the United States and finds himself peerless in his insight.

To remain adept, Kelly perpetually studies the major domestic issues of our time and examines and reexamines potential sensible solutions. He ran for U.S. Congress as a Democrat in 2010, adhering to his vow to take no campaign donations in 2010 and was pleased to receive 17% of the vote despite being vastly outspent and having little prior name recognition.

He understood the system to be rigged against ordinary Americans like himself who are not indentured to a major donor with plenty of reserve funds and harbored no illusions of overnight success. Kelly is not for purchase; his merit lies in diagnosis and rectification of problems.

Increasingly, more Democrats such as Brian are beginning to realize that the entrenched class, also known as "the Swamp," has control over everything consequential in the U.S. except for the often-misdirected voting power of the people. Though we still retain control of the government to some extent, we often fail to correctly exercise our power. Kelly believes that even the few crumbs and inches gained are only acquired once those gains have been predetermined by the powers to be worthless. Like many of you, he opposes our domination by this Swamp.

Like Donald Trump, your author wants to make America great again. Not being president of course, makes it a lot more difficult to insert real solutions into the political mix of today. Brian Kelly is your average normal guy but for one difference. In his role as the most published non-fiction author in America, Kelly has built a solution for each of the most pressing domestic US issues of today.

For each problem, Kelly has at least one book in his arsenal that solves the problem. Sometimes it takes two and sometimes even more than two books to completely solve the most nagging issues.

Brian Kelly writes, and he writes, and he thinks, and he articulates. But, as a normal, regular American; he has no power or resources to force his ideas upon anyone. It is not an easy task.

Even Donald Trump as CEO of America is having problems dislodging the gunk and muck in the Swamp and getting his agenda implemented. The Swamp dwellers have lots of spare cash to fight all comers. The Establishment has many people to whom they pay large sums to fight for them every day. For that, the political junkies in the SWAMP get the best advice about how to keep the President at bay.

Brian Kelly's major domestic solutions are contained in his books. Ten books in the larger edition of this immigration effort, unfortunately to solve ten major problems provides a lot of material for solutions. Consequently, it is too much reading all at once for even the best of us. And, so, the purpose of the "Whitman's Sampler" book of synopses, and this, a slice of that book dedicated just to immigration issues is set to be a book of books, written in "CliffsNotes" style for easy reading and comprehending.

The book [As from which SOLVED has evolved] is titled: *Top Ten American Political Books for 2018*. It provides a comprehensive set of summaries on the best approaches to tackle the major domestic US issues that we are facing in 2018. It is designed to be read one chapter at a time in a short period so that Americans can have a big win for the country. When the right people read this set of "CliffsNotes" books and begin to pass laws and implement the plans contained herein, America will be well on its way to greatness again, working to achieve independence from those keeping us down.

Brian Kelly is not a total cynic but a realist like many lifelong Democrats whose disgust with established special interests has made them gravitate towards the countermeasure of Donald Trump. Why should ordinary people volunteer to be pushed around by dishonest Democrats anymore? Despite being a billionaire, Trump relates to the people in a way that breaks through the authoritarian forced politeness behind which masquerades the nefarious interests of the entrenched political class.

Donald Trump takes no salary as he finds being a great president as reward enough for his daily toil. Even as he is constantly assailed by our disingenuous and certifiably fake news media, he dusts himself off and goes right back at it the next day on behalf of all of us.

Democrats have failed their original vision of a world where families can earn a decent wage by working, opting instead to reward their anti-American donors who prey on the very people the Party was founded to help prosper. Democrats want the people to believe that their captured government should be sufficient for the people's needs, having done their best to extinguish any members who otherwise would be driven to work on behalf of the population at large.

One of the greatest challenges President Trump faces is how to rehabilitate faith in our system, when the Democratic Party, a once reliable bedrock institution, is now bitterly distrusted. We all wish him well on that account.

So, what does someone without Mr. Trump's resources do? Most of us cannot afford to run a successful campaign but are united in our goal of *Making America Great Again*. Kelly hopes his ideas can influence the nation and President Trump personally, as though they both lack pure omniscience, they share a powerful intellect, heart of gold, and desire to restore America to its former glory.

Kelly has some great ideas. He increasingly sells more and more books each month but because he currently lacks fame, his solutions have yet to reach a widespread audience that could one day promote the policies that ultimately reach the President's desk. He writes, thinks, and articulates, knowing full well that his ideas' path to fruition is an indirect one. While Mr. Trump has the power and influence to accomplish many of his plans for the nation, Brian understands that his ideas are going nowhere unless they are put into action prompted by popular will and executed by the President's pen.

As noted previously, the road ahead is difficult. Even Donald Trump himself is having problems dislodging the sludge and serpentine slugs in the dreaded swamp who have full control of America. They are able to spare any expense to protect their system of chicanery at all costs, including paid lackeys in the media who defend the indefensible.

They are well organized and protected. Another lever in the system of revolving doors include the overpaid consultants who provide inside access to electoral success. For many of the most venal knaves in office purporting to be public servants, re-election of course is a vanity success for its own sake, rather than enabling a better life for the citizens of this country.

So, what does Brian Kelly have to offer? This book provides a good overview. Titled *Top Ten American Political Books for 2018*, it is a synopsis on the best approaches to tackle domestic US issues in 2018 for Americans to finally achieve success in the country.

Nothing in life worth having is easy and the only thing once can do alone in life is fail. And, so, Brian Kelly has had a good friend for the last six years, Congressman Lou Barletta who also hails from Northeastern Pennsylvania and currently serves as its representative. Kelly and Barletta became friends when Kelly ran for Congress, lost in the primary, and asked Barletta how he could help him win his Congressional seat.

Kelly continually communicates with and meets with the Congressman to discuss his ideas for the improvement America. The Congressman is always warm and engaging and Kelly hopes to demonstrate enough popular political will to move forward with his policy ideas. Kelly believes the Congressman is the real deal, so to speak, so he continues to raise awareness of these issues in his presence as he believes it to be one of the best avenues to reach President Trump.

Brian supports this Congressman in 2018 for his next big strategic operation—a run for the US Senate. Pennsylvania currently has one of the ineptest Senators representing the state in Pennsylvania history. Bob Casey Jr. a nice enough guy from Scranton, is regarded as but a shadow of the towering figure his father was, when the senior Casey served as Governor of Pennsylvania.

Most people in the local area gave up hope on Casey Jr. a long time ago, as he revealed himself to be little more than a water-carrier for Barack Obama and then Hillary Clinton in her notoriously corrupt failed bid for President in 2016.

To put Casey in perspective, when he first ran for the U.S. Senate, a Philadelphia Inquirer columnist wrote that Casey's *make-no-waves style* was as exciting as "oatmeal." Considering the Inquirer's center-left editorial bias, the fact that this was the most positive thing they could muster was a surprise to even Democrats.

Brian Kelly wrote this new compendium book so that between the covers of just one book, he is now able to introduce the precepts that are detailed in all ten books released in 2017. In this way, policy makers and interested citizens alike can have an even more concise tool from which to create the legislation necessary to disinfect the United States of the major issues that are keeping the country from moving forward without impediment.

By way of a list, as a topical introduction, these are the major domestic issues for which Brian Kelly has fashioned the most appropriate solutions for 2008.

- ✓ Saving millennials so they do not become the lost generation
- ✓ Refranchise student borrowers
- ✓ Prescribes how colleges and universities can become more honest in promising the world to 17-year-old high school kids, and locking them in to huge debt
- ✓ Remove welfare as a free lunch
- ✓ Ending healthcare redistribution
- ✓ Provide Social Security recipients with a COLA that makes up for past inaccuracies
- ✓ Provide a no-amnesty, no cost, pro-American rescue of illegal aliens from the shadows.
- ✓ Provide cash for self-deportation of illegal aliens
- ✓ Provide cash for self-deportation of anchor babies
- ✓ Provide cash for self-deportation of two-term green card holders.
- ✓ Provide no amnesty; no way!
- ✓ Provide a system so that Americans have first opportunities for every job that comes available.
- ✓ Save well over $500 billion per year on immigration costs
- ✓ Repeal Obamacare with a market, not a government replacement.
- ✓ Downsize the EPA by 95%
- ✓ Avoid Taxation Without Representation

The solutions written in the latter part of 2017 are contained in Brian Kelly's ten books that are outlined in this book titled, *Top Ten American Political Books for 2018* and the solutions are primed to help America with its domestic problem set for 2018.   The books are listed in reverse order of publishing date. The book titles contain solutions for all of the above listed problems.

The Top Ten Political Books in America for 2018 are as follows:

- Taxation Without Representation Fourth Edition--Can the U.S. Avoid Another "Boston Tea Party?"
- DELETE the EPA! EPA agenda is not to save human lives. Is its insidious goal world population control?
- Deport All Millennials Now! It ought to be easy. They'll line up like it's a free vacation
- No Free Lunch—Pay Back Welfare The first book that recommends that welfare should not be free money
- Wipe Out All Student Debt Now! Unique solutions to the $1.45 Trillion debt accumulation
- Boost Social Security Now! A solution to get Seniors out of the poorhouse; Hey buddy, can you spare a dime?
- Legalizing Illegal Aliens Via Resident Visas-- A great Americans-first plan which saves $Trillions. Learn how!
- Pay-To-Go-- An America-first immigration fix No more deportations
- Obamacare: A One-Line Repeal Congress must get this done
- 60 Million Illegals in America!!! A simple, America-first solution!

Of course, this book, SOLVED, is a subset of the subset for those who are interested in solving the problem of 60 million illegal residents in the USA. Thank you for paying attention toone of the most important issue of our times. Should America stay America. As Nancy Pelosi says, why should Whitey Americans not want the browns or the blacks to become dominant? Why are Whitey's acting like white supremacist racist when it would be much better to give up the country to the browns? That kinda talk disgusts me. How about you?

Do you think Nancy is right?

Is something wrong with white if that happens to be who you are, through no fault of your own? Sounds like tyranny of the minority!

Thank you,
Brian Patrick Kelly
Editor in Chief & Publisher of Lets Go Publish! Publishers.

Chapter 8 Legalizing Illegal Aliens via Resident Visas

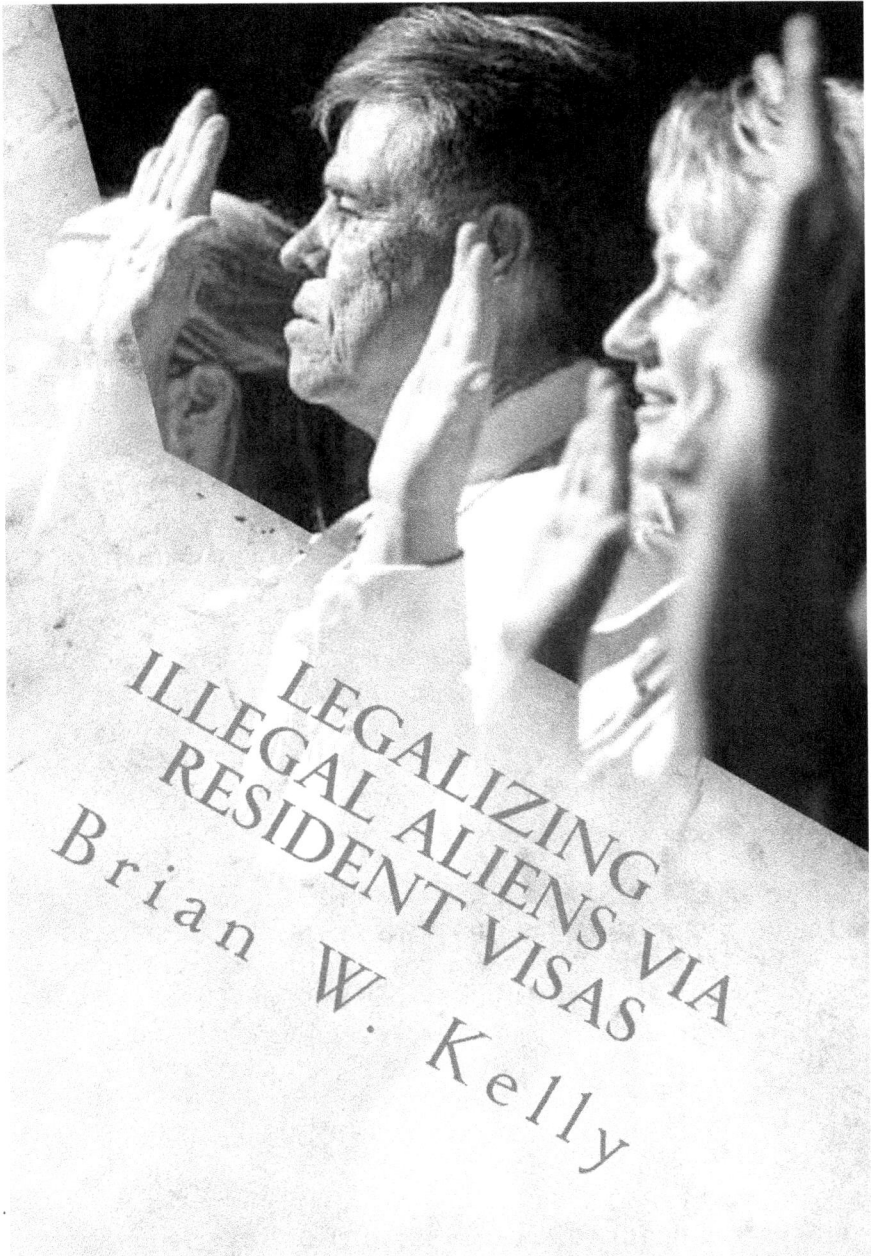

A great Americans-first plan which saves $Trillions. Learn how!

Book purpose:

Despite our best efforts pre-Obama, for the 32 years after the 1986 Reagan Amnesty, the flow of interlopers across the border and from visa overstayers brought in from 1 million to 4 million illegal aliens per year. That means anywhere from 32 million to 128 million found homes in America during this period. It is a national crisis.

Obama's lax immigration policies in which he basically told our Border Patrols to stand down made matters even worse over the last eight years.

Meanwhile, many Americans forgot they once had jobs and they began to believe that their depressed wages caused by illegal immigration would never abate. Democrats convinced them that maybe it was their fault.

Former president Obama took no action in eight years to protect Americans and so when President Trump ran for President, there were already many who had been affected negatively and they voted for Trump en-masse. They hoped that the flow of illegal foreign nationals would stop and that we could deport those who had entered illegally.

Liberals try to convince Americans that there are just 11 million illegal foreign interlopers, but nobody is buying it. The same song has been played for the last twenty years. John McCain's estimate is 128 million and my own estimate is 60 million. These people live in the shadows, take American jobs, and for each one on welfare, they cost US taxpayers about $30,000 per year. The total is about $500,000,000,000 per year and the effect on low wages and few available on Americans is another $500,000,000,000 per year. It has to stop now.

Despite the toll on our country, most Americans see deporting 60 million or even 11 million foreigners as cruel and unusual punishment. At least that is what the crooked press wants us to believe. I wrote this book because I have a better idea. We can legalize all of the 60 million after a comprehensive in-person vetting process and a first-year fee of $200.00 and $100.00 in each subsequent year.

If the interlopers agree to the provisos and are approved after vetting, the one-time interlopers would receive an annually renewable new type of visa, called a resident visa.

To gain and keep their resident visa status the interlopers would promise to take no welfare and no free healthcare and no freebies of any kind. If they don't take our offer, and they do not take the Pay-to-Go offer, they will be deported.

They must have their own or employer provided healthcare. They can keep their current jobs, but all Americans would be considered first in line for any new jobs. Additionally, they must promise never to vote in any American election and unless they go back to their home countries, they can never get in line for citizenship.

No Sanctuary Cities or DACA needed

There would no longer be a need for sanctuary cities, and the DACA problem would be solved for each of the "DACA people" who are approved for the resident visa. There is lots more. The major benefit for illegals is that they are out of the shadows and the major benefit for Americans is that they are first for jobs and the country saves about $500 billion in welfare costs each year.

The notion of a resident visa permits us to solve the problem of 60 million interlopers without any deportations other than for criminals and unsavory characters. It is a permanent program that puts Americans first in all matters. It is such a good idea that it can actually replace the green card and the notion of anchor babies. Instead of birthright citizenship, anchor babies would get a resident visa with no welfare.

What today are green card holders, would get a special resident visa as a citizen designator if they otherwise would have qualified for a green card. If they are not citizens within the ten-year designation, they would lose the citizen aspirant designation. No illegal foreign national legalized under this program would be eligible for a citizen aspirant designation.

What if a current interloper does not want to give up welfare benefits. Such a person can sign up for a companion program covered in a book titled, Pay-to-Go. A stipend of from $20,000 to $50,000 plus transportation costs will be paid to anybody in former illegal status or in green card status or anchor baby status. They can take a nice bundle of cash to their home country with each family member receiving a substantial amount. Their families can be reunited in their home countries with enough proceeds to become successful entrepreneurs.

Democrats still want the interloper vote

Everybody knows that the objective of the left during the Obama presidency was to get as many illegal foreign nationals into the country as possible. Into the country for when the big amnesty comes, Republicans won't be able to get elected as dog-catcher.

The Atlantic argues that this is a new position of the Democrats who once were for regular Americans, but now are for every group on the fringe and are no longer nationalistic in perspective. Here is what they say in a piece written in 2017:

"In 2005, a left-leaning blogger wrote, "Illegal immigration wreaks havoc economically, socially, and culturally; makes a mockery of the rule of law; and is disgraceful just on basic fairness grounds alone." In 2006, a liberal columnist wrote that "immigration reduces the wages of domestic workers who compete with immigrants" and that "the fiscal burden of low-wage immigrants is also pretty clear." His conclusion: "We'll need to reduce the inflow of low-skill immigrants."

"That same year, a Democratic senator wrote, "When I see Mexican flags waved at pro-immigration demonstrations, I sometimes feel a flush of patriotic resentment. When I'm forced to use a translator to communicate with the guy fixing my car, I feel a certain frustration.""

The blogger was Glenn Greenwald. The columnist was Paul Krugman. The senator was Barack Obama. See how much they have changed. Today, even these three champions of the left would have their Democrat cards pulled for uttering such speak.

Americans have not changed. We are still not at all happy about any amnesty. Thus, no solution for the 60 million interlopers living freely in the shadows of America with no fear under former president Obama-style protections can come without Americans being the winners.

The Resident Visa Program as proposed in this book takes a hard look at Americans who do not want to deport illegals en masse yet want the country back under full American control. Foreign Nationals should have no say and certainly no vote. Looking at the reality of our times, it is time to offer Americans a solution to the 60 million residents that we can live with and with which, all Americans can prosper.

The reported sentiment is that nobody in America but a few of the unsavory variety, want the stain of deportation on their own souls. If this is true, this problem solves that issue. Regardless, the programs revealed in this book can solve the resident interloper problem in a pro-American way without requiring coerced deportations for non-criminals. Let's get criminals out as quickly as possible.

Even liberals ten years ago recognized that the border-hopping low-skilled immigrants depressed the wages of low-skilled entry level American workers and strained America's welfare state. No kidding! But, something happened between then and now. In 2008, the Democratic Party platform called undocumented immigrants "our neighbors, but it still offered some cautions. By 2016, the immigration section of the platform didn't use the word illegal, or any variation of it, at all. The former illegals had become future voters. This really upsets Americans who pay more than lip-service to America. Why the change?

The brutal truth is that illegal aliens vote, and in large numbers. Though the corrupt press mocked President Trump when he pointed this out after his election, it is true. Voter fraud is not exclusive to illegal aliens, however. There are also legal aliens (green card, H1B visas, tourist visa holders, etc.) who vote illegally. Democrats are very pleased to look the other way.

What do Americans want? Check out the list of the top five items that Americans want before they would agree to any form of legalization.

1. Only Americans vote
2. No welfare for non-citizens. That means no free cash, medical services, education, or welfare services / benefits.
3. Employers must hire American citizens first
4. No amnesty or citizenship
5. Must speak English

The Resident Visa Program (RVP) as proposed in this book provides these assurances for Americans. For an illegal foreign national to be granted such a visa, they would be required to swear that they agree 100% with the five items Americans care most about as well as others that would be part of a total resident visa package.

One at a time, candidates for the program would pay $200 each to be vetted. If accepted, they would gain a one-year residence pass known as a resident visa, paperwork, and an ID card with biometrics that must be kept on their person at all times. Their visa would be renewable every year for $100.00 as long as they remain model residents, a term which will be defined to mean all aspects of "keeping their noses clean."

This visa is intended to take all illegal foreign nationals out of the shadows and into the light of day. There may also be some fines and fees for having broken American law that can be paid "on account."

The cost savings for Americans are immense.

No analyst estimate on the cost of illegal aliens is below $100 billion per year. When all of the services are totaled up, there are estimates of cost savings higher than $500 billion. America can save $500 billion or more per year in direct costs by enacting this legislation.

Additionally, there are studies that demonstrate the costs that are born by Americans per year for illegal foreign nationals lowering wages and taking the jobs of Americans. These are estimated at another $500 billion per year.

It would not take even five years for most of these dollars to begin to flow in America's favor. This is a big economic deal for Americans. Since to be approved, Resident Visa Holders must agree to a "no freebies" clause in the contract, I would suggest a two-year, non-extendable, continuation of existing benefits for those already on welfare. After that, former interlopers would either pay their own way to keep the visa or select the Pay-to-Go option explained in this mini-book.

Side Benefit: DACA & Sanctuary Cities Solved

Among other things, this automatically solves the DACA problem and the sanctuary city problem. No sanctuaries are necessary when everybody can be legal and productive in the USA. As a concession to Democrats, DACA "children" should have their annual renewal fee canceled for ten years, but they still must renew each year. as all other resident visa holders.

Additionally, different forms of the Resident Visa can be created so that we can do away with all of the benefits such as welfare that come with green cards. There would be substantial cost savings there. Rather than ten-year renewable permanent residents in line for citizenship, those who would be green card holders under today's program would become Resident Visa holders instead and those in the green card program would change to resident visa holder at their ten-year renewal. This special visa form would permit citizenship.

No former illegal alien who becomes a resident visa holder under this program would ever be able to change status to get in line for citizenship. Only by going back to the home country and approaching it legally from there would this be possible.

I wrote another book titled *Pay-to-Go*, which is also examined in the Top Ten book from which this book was extracted. *Pay-to-Go* demonstrates the major cost savings that would accrue to the US by providing huge stipends as high as $20,000 for illegals who agree to permanently depart the US for their home country.

Restricting their access to welfare has been a principle of American domestic policy since colonial times. The federal law, established in 1882 and strengthened in the early twentieth century, was that immigration officials should refuse entry to any non-citizen who appeared likely to become a "public charge" and should deport those who did, although actual deportations of public charges have been rare. When a sitting president suggests that ICE look the other way on illegal non-citizens, it makes our laws a sham and makes America the caretaker of all the world's poor.

The Obama Agriculture Department blatantly solicited food stamp recipients from among the illegal population.

A Spanish-language leaflet was created in 2013 that the U.S. Department of Agriculture has provided to the Mexican Embassy in Washington advises border-crossing Mexicans that they can collect taxpayer-funded food stamp benefits for their children without admitting that they're illegal immigrants.

Underlined and in boldface type, the document tells immigrants who are unlawfully in the United States that, 'You need not divulge information regarding your immigration status in seeking this benefit for your children.'

While other countries are reducing what they will give to foreigners living legally in their countries, the US gives as much to foreigners as to Americans. No wonder they come here illegally when there is no enforcement of anything. For example, After a recent meeting on the National Immigration and Integration, French Interior Minister Manuel Valls announced significant changes in the country's migration policy. The government will reduce financial assistance to immigrants, and this reduction will be substantial. Starting March 1, French immigrant benefits will be cut by 83 percent.

America is not the only country in this bind of having too many residents from foreign countries who are on the public dole, though America pays the top amount to foreigners living here legally and illegally.

Countries as far away as Australia have problems with migrants taking native jobs. They use a technique called the Assisted Voluntary Return as part of an overall Pay-to-Go plan to incent migrants to leave Australia and return back home. They are OK with these migrants going home with or without Aussie assistance. As noted, one of the books you will take a peek at in this book is titled, "Pay-to-Go." That book explains it all.

This notion, which is not an American idea, across the globe, pays both travel expenses and offers a generous stipend for those in potential despair who sign up for the offer to return home. Then, they arrive home with a lot of bucks in their individual pockets. They get to start businesses, and take care of their families and for them, the American dream helped to deposit them in their home country with a wad of cash that they could not have gained by themselves in a million years. Once home, they are entitled to use their stipends to prosper with their families. Should life be so good for everybody?

But, then in America, there are those who do not wish to leave. What about these? They have no interest to leave the USA no matter what the incentive may be? Should they be left behind when the boat pulls out for their home countries? Maybe so! Maybe not! But this is America not their homeland and we must always be for Americans first.

Are we Americans better off with the remainder of 60 million illegal interlopers staying in the shadows of America, rather than devising a plan to solve the problem in a way that keeps America whole and makes Americans the masters of our own country again?

The last official try by eight corrupt US Senators to right this wrong was called the Gang-of-Eight plan and it basically gave up America and Americans for the benefit of the illegal interlopers. It put them on a fast track to citizenship that would cost US taxpayers up to $6.3 Trillion with all of its provisions. In 2013, Americans told Congress nyet, and the House voted "no" and we sent the Gang of Eight Senators packing but they still are hanging around.

Unfortunately, if we do nothing to end the tremendous cost and sacrifice of accommodating the 60 million illegal interlopers in the shadows of the USA, we cannot sustain our resolve to be free again of oppressive congressional actions.

Will this scurrilous gang of 8 re-emerge and take Americans down? How long can we Americans withstand this situation, which many rightfully call A Mexican Standoff. Our country is clearly in chaos. We see a race to the bottom in wages that is underway; and regular Americans suffer by losing the jobs and low-wages war every day.

Meanwhile, there is no American consensus as Democrat-dominated American cities and certain Democrat states have decided to offer sanctuary to illegal foreigners rather than to American patriots. They choose not to support the needs of American citizens. The point is that if we Americans opt to do nothing, this real standoff in the USA is scheduled never to end. Democrats have chosen to stand against regular Americans who love America.

The one clear choice for those wishing to stay in America would be if we can legalize interlopers with no benefits at all. This would end the sanctuaries and the shadows and be good for everybody. I think we can do it. That is what this book is about.

In this book, you can read about how to legalize Illegal Aliens via a new notion called a resident visa. It takes interlopers out of the shadows and gives them the opportunity they seek while keeping Americans whole and keeping the country prospering with Americans in charge. You're going to like this America-first plan built by an American for Americans,

Brian W. Kelly

Preface:

What would you call a plan that solved a problem for America that most of the Congress seem to have no interest in solving? I have called it many things while perfecting this book, but now let me settle my mental rumblings with what it should be called The Resident Visa Plan. It has a companion plan called the Pay-to-Go Plan, another book that is highlighted later in this book.

Legalizing Illegal Aliens Via Resident Visas is the first book of two recently introduced. Together, both books fully address the solution to 60 million interlopers residing in America. The second book, that has been released is the companion book. Its title is Pay-To-Go.

Both of these books should be required reading for every House and Senate member as well as the President of the United States. Together, these are the only plans that can work for Americans-first—to end the shadows and the sanctuaries and save America about a $Trillion per year. Both books are available on the Amazon and Barnes & Noble sites.

The Resident Visa Plan is a vision for a secret sauce solution to fix the problem of 60 million interlopers waking up in America every day without our permission. Yes—build the wall, please! But simultaneously solve the residence problem of so many people who do not belong here in America.

What American believes that we really need up to 60 million interlopers in residence? I do not think so. Hey, John McCain thinks there are over 128 million interlopers in residence. Maybe he is right. Do we need 128 Million? Can anybody tell me what we need? My personal thoughts say we need zero illegals. It is time to give Americans an opportunity to work in America.

I am very pleased that you are reading this book and I hope many others find it and convince the US Administration and the Congress and the President that it is their turn to learn about The Resident Visa Plan. It should have been obvious without me, a guy from no place giving the Congress and the President such a good idea, but I am very pleased to do so.

The Resident Visa solution is unique, and everything needed to implement it is already in place. It directly addresses the issues that having 60 million illegal foreign nationals in residence have brought upon America. Nobody likes deportation but just like you would throw an uninvited guest out of your house, it would be very fair for the US to throw out (deport) the 60 million uninvited guests in America today.

Yes, deportation is fair of course as these folks have broken our laws. But, our politicians are culpable as they made it too easy for foreigners to break our laws. The problem is that we do not see them in our house every day and so most of us have no stomach for deporting them.

Therefore, an adjunct solution to the Resident Visa Plan is a Pay-to-Go Plan. The US will pay the return expenses for each illegal interloper who chooses to return to their home country. Moreover, depending on their status in the USA, the government will provide a generous stipend of anywhere from $20,000 to $50,000 once they return. That's a good deal.

Amnesty is not a solution as Americans have already paid a big price for the largesse of politicians wanting low wages and those wanting the future votes of today's interlopers.

Ideally, the solution would be to go poof, and every foreign interloper would be taken back to where and when they crossed the border years and years ago.

Every plan requires fine tuning and we would expect this to continue to be the case with the Resident Visa Plan. When illegal interlopers do not want to be paid to go, and they want to stay in the US, the Resident Visa Plan comes in very handy. Together these plans are the long-sought solution to 60 million illegals in America. Nobody will be illegal and there will be no need for sanctuary citizens.

Instead of birthright citizens, those born in the US with resident visa parents would automatically become resident visa holders with the yearly fee waived until they hit 21-years of age.

A key element of this plan is that each year the clock resets on foreign nationals who are permitted here on a temporary basis under the Resident Visa Plan. This book, thus focuses on interlopers signing up to become Resident Visa Holders with appropriate renewal assurances for good behavior.

In summary, this book presents the Resident Visa Plan as the fix and the Pay-to-Go Plan as the backup fix. Then it offers many other points on why this is the one and only fix to create an America without shadows that favors Americans 100%. There is so much good left over that good-willed interlopers have a lot to gain simply by signing up.

You are going to love this book as well as the plans themselves. All interlopers immediately are to be registered and accountable. You will see that The Resident Visa Plan is designed by an American for Americans idea whose time has come.

Additionally, illegal foreign nationals will be very pleased because the plan uses deportation as a very last resort and it immediately gets illegal foreign nationals out of the shadows. Few books are a must-read, but this highlighted book and The Resident Visa Plan will quickly appear at the top of America's most read list.

This is a simple, America-first solution but only if Congress and the President have the guts! It solves the problem with 60 million interlopers in America and many others!

Table of Contents

Ch 1 Is There a Solution?
60 million interlopers cost taxpayer dollars

If we knew how to immediately stop the drain on our government treasury with one bold and very fair move, would America's inept politicians make that move? I have done many analyses and I have concluded that American politicians, from Congress and the Senate on down. will never support Americans unless convinced that they would be out of office otherwise.

Based on what it costs to support illegal foreign nationals (average of $30,000 per person per year), the US can certainly afford to deport millions of people. But, the dirty politicians and the corrupt press preach a different mantra that puts Americans last and illegal aliens first.

Ironically, though Americans complain about all of the illegal aliens, supporting them, having them take their jobs, and lowering the average wages in America, most would prefer a different solution than rounding them up and deporting 60 million people. But, we can afford deportation if we choose. If nobody was collecting welfare, this would be a lot tougher, and if nobody in illegal status was stealing from Americans, maybe no American would care.

Can we afford a mass deportation of illegal foreign nationals—even without a roundup?

Is there a consensus for or against the idea? It only matters if the US can actually afford to undertake a mass deportation?

Let me prove that we can afford deportation before we move on to solutions that we can stomach. I am not recommending mass deportation, but we can certainly afford it and the US can save lots of money if we chose to do it.

Let's say that 30 million of the 60 million illegal aliens in residence collect some form of welfare from the US to help afford their lives in America. What does that cost us per year?

The cost per year is $30,000 X 30,000,000 = $900 Billion per year
The cost of deportation is $10,000 X 30 million = $300 Billion one time

The first-year savings is a net of $600 Billion after deportation. The second and subsequent years, the savings would be the full $900 Billion per year

Rather than look at the unpleasant task of coerced deportation, many countries across the world have instituted what they call Pay-to-Go programs in which a free return and a stipend incentive are offered to the migrants to induce them to return home. In our country we would be incenting illegal interlopers living in the shadows of America.

A very nice stipend amount that would persuade many interlopers to return to their home country is $20,000. In this way, the deportation is really a voluntary emigration back to the home country.

The cost of the stipend at $20,000 X 30,000,000 = $600 Billion one time. This is if the country is the USA.

In this example, the cost of the return and the cost of the stipend would be $900 billion if every interloper agreed to return home and then executed on their promise.

This is the same amount as the cost to support all interlopers in the US for one year. The difference between the two is the savings. In year 1, in this scenario, the savings would be zero dollars and the cost would be zero dollars. In year two an annual savings of $900 billion would begin to accrue. Where does the savings come from? It comes from the US not having to pay welfare to illegals as well as Americans being able to get jobs that pay substantially more than when the interlopers were depressing wages by accepting sub-minimum wage positions. .

Suppose the Pay-to-Go stipend were raised to $50,000, to attract more takers, the annual savings of as much as $900 billion would begin to accrue in year three so the stipend could be paid for. After year three, the US is in the black on the program.

Talk to your Congress

I predict that the biggest obstacle in solving the problem of 60 million illegal interlopers in America will be both chambers of the US Congress. I am not naïve enough to suggest that the current Congress' predilection for more voters and lower wages for all Americans could be overcome by the fact that this plan to deal with resident interlopers is the best yet conceived. So, if they remain recalcitrant, we may be forced to replace the entire Congress in order to do the right thing for America.

John McCain is known for his personal estimate of about 4 million per year jumping the border. He is talking about Illegal aliens, which we like to refer to as illegal interlopers. An interloper is another word for an uninvited guest.

McCain's estimate is of those who have chosen to cross the southern border. In his estimate, he does not include the million or more a year who simply decide not to go home when their visas expire. Instead they opt for illegal residency in the US. That's how we got into this problem in the first place. We did not invite 60 million people to America to sponge off US taxpayers. However, some of our elite representatives may very well have done exactly that.

US. amnesty advocate John McCain, is a recognized authority on the subject of illegal immigration. In a letter dated February 2004, he wrote that apprehension figures demonstrated that "almost four million people crossed the US border illegally in 2002."

McCain estimates over 10,000 cross every day. If it were exactly 10,000, then 3,650,000 per year would be his estimate. Instead he simply rounded it up to 4 million. That comes to 128 million from 1986, the year of the Reagan amnesty to the end of 2017. If we cut that in half and round it down, we're looking at my long-time estimate of 60 million interlopers in residence today. I know that nobody can prove me wrong on that number.

...

What about legal immigration?

About 1.2 million green cards are expected to be issued in 2017. In 2014, a total of 1,016,518 persons became lawful permanent residents—aka, LPRs complete with green card status. Over half of the new LPRs (53 percent) already lived in the United States when they were granted lawful permanent residence. Sixty-four percent of the new LPRs were granted lawful permanent resident status based on a family relationship with a U.S. citizen or lawful permanent resident of the United States. The leading countries of birth of new LPRs were Mexico (13 percent), India (7.7 percent), and China (7.5 percent)

The other type of legal resident in the US is known as a birthright citizen, colloquially known as an anchor baby.

If the stipend is a little higher, the Pay-to-Go Program could save the US another ton of funds if it were also used to attract green card holders on welfare, and anchor babies on welfare. When and if they agreed to return to their home countries there would no longer be a cost for their welfare. Think of what the US could do with another half trillion or as much as a full trillion dollars per year to spend on American interests?

The three categories for which the program could be used in the future include the following:

1. Current interlopers
2. Legal green card holders on welfare
3. Anchor babies at any age, including children supervised by a legal or illegal parent.

The recommended stipend for each of the three categories would be as follows:

1. Current Interlopers $20,000
2. Legal Green Card Holders on Welfare $30,000
3. Anchor Babies or Adults $50,000

Anybody opting for a stipend in any of the above categories would be prohibited without special petition from ever returning to the United States for any reason. Any debt accrued that is accounted for in the Accountability system, explained in Chapter 17. would need to be collected prior to any request for readmission to be examined.

There are 15 million legal immigrants (green card holders) currently in the country. Half of them are on welfare. 7.5 million X $30,000 = $225 Billion per year. There are 6 million birthright citizens (former anchor babies) born to illegal aliens currently in the country. They are almost all on welfare 6 million X $30,000 = $180 Billion per year

The US can thus save an additional $405 Billion per year by adding the above two categories to the illegal interlopers able to use the Pay-to Go program or any other program that reduces costs to zero. This would make a total of three categories for which the program could be used.

What problem does the Pay-to Go program fix? It is a pro-America and pro-American citizen solution. It is an America-First solution to the major problem of 60 million illegal residents sponging off the taxpayers in the United States.

Once in the continental US, the interlopers either wholly or partially depend on US taxpayer dollars for their daily sustenance. Is your wallet looking a little thinner these days? The problem we plan to solve in this book, the real problem, is that 60 million illegal foreign nationals cost Americans money every day. They just don't pay their way and live here. They take from US.

Chapter 9 Pay-to-Go

Pay-to-Go

America-First Immigration Fix

Brian W. Kelly

America-First Immigration Fix

Book purpose:

In Chapter 8, Legalizing Illegal Aliens Via Resident Visas, we discussed the purpose of a plan that legalizes illegal aliens who choose to stay in America with conditions that include no vote, no welfare, no citizenship, etc. In the beginning of the chapter, we presented a summary of the plan.

This book, Pay-to-Go, with a plan of the same name, Pay-to-Go, is a companion program to the Resident Visa Plan. It has many of the same purposes. The difference between the two major plans is that under Pay-to-Go, illegal foreign nationals choose not to stay in America. Instead, they go back to their home countries for good. To help them out when they get home, the US provides them full transportation costs plus a stipend from $20,000 to $50,000 depending on their status:

1. Illegal Alien
2. Green Card
3. Anchor Baby.

After a year or so, based on the cost of welfare, and the size of the stipend, the US government under Pay-to-Go will save $30,000 for each person who takes this deal. If everybody took the deal, this would save the US over $500 billion per year. Similar savings are achieved for those who choose to stay in America under the Resident Visa Plan.

Most illegal foreign national live with welfare support

Illegal immigrants living in the shadows use stolen and fake IDs to survive. It is a fact. It is much easier than you would think for those in the hidden economy of the US to gain welfare benefits including healthcare. Hospital social services departments are motivated to sign illegals up for Medicaid rather than absorb the EMTALA (ER) costs themselves. The estimated cost per illegal on welfare is $30,000 per year. That is a lot of money.

The fake news estimate for how many illegals live in America is about 11 million. Donald Trump estimates the number at 30 million. However, if we consider that since 1986, thirty-two years ago, from one to three million per year have crossed our borders without documentation.

That means that by all accounts, we have between 32 million to 96 million foreign interlopers scratching a living from the shadows using fake ids, welfare, and whatever means possible to survive. John McCain has estimated that there are 128 million foreign interlopers in America today. So, for a reality check, let's just say the number is closer to 60 million than 11 million. Yet, our statistics systems are so poor that nobody really knows.

There are estimates that the US welfare agencies at various levels as well as health agencies and school systems spend as much as $500 billion per year taking care of illegal foreigners. Considering that as many as half of the green card holders, who are permanent legal immigrants are on the welfare dole in one way or another. The costs to American taxpayers are staggering.

If we permitted all such residents who wanted to go home to go home all expenses paid, and we gave them $20,000 to as much as $50,000 in the form of a stipend to leave, in as little as one year or as many as three years, the US would have a net gain of as much as $500 billion per year thereafter. It would cost us nothing and after a short while, we would be $500 billion to the good each year.

Of course, not all those eligible would opt to leave so we would need another program such as a Resident Visa Plan, described in another book. To handle those who choose to stay in the country legally and agree not to accept benefits.

When you read this book, you will find that the biggest problem with 60,000,000 interlopers in America is that your friendly representative in Congress does not respect your concerns for America. Americans must send home their representatives as they no longer represent the people.

How is it possible that 60 million illegal aliens are living today in America and Congress is not even talking about it? Well, Congress invited them here as sure as they are seated in the Capitol of the country every day doing nothing to help their constituents.

As difficult as it is for good, hard-working Americans to believe, our government has been working to keep us poor. Former President Obama's de-facto amnesties and a do-nothing Congress made it tough for Americans to find work while competing against these foreign interlopers.

Congress has been lying, and yet their efforts have produced a terrible truth—Americans have been left behind and nobody cares. Meanwhile, uninvited guests, working for peanuts, have reduced wages and taken the few jobs that exist today. After they get here, these poor souls languish in misery and a lifetime of poverty as even what they take from our welfare system is hardly enough.

Pay-to-Go is used in countries all over the world, including Australia, to pay foreign workers or foreign interlopers to go home expenses paid and often with a generous stipend. Pay-to-Go needs to be implemented in America. The plan would be to help Americans-first and it would be designed to help illegal foreign nationals in residence to have a much better life with cash in their pockets in their home countries. With this plan, they will no longer be chained to greedy businesses looking for slave-labor wages.

Those who sign up for the program will have a chance to go home and enjoy life with a huge stipend that actually pays for itself. Not only would it cost Americans nothing after a few years, it would provide a lot of dollars to the treasury. There's lots more! You're going to like this America-first plan built by an American for Americans! Talk to your representative to make sure this plan passes in the Congress.

Preface:

In this book, we provide arguments that 60 million illegal aliens in our one-time All-American Country is a problem for the US to sustain. The arguments are both cultural / social and financial. Analysts have presented the case that the yearly cost for supporting so many foreign nationals on our dime is between $500 billion and $1.5 trillion per year and it is growing each year as interlopers just love our eighty odd welfare programs.

There are so many social programs that even after reviewing them multiple times, even I cannot recite them from memory. Nobody can figure out why we have so many welfare programs. But, the illegal foreign nationals are well versed on them all when they come to live in America. There is much redundancy and many programs could be eliminated or replaced without altering the needs addressed. But that is a topic for another day.

Nonetheless, the foreign interloper of today lives in the shadows and he or she understands enough English to be able to know the welfare regulations in the US. Those interlopers with major English skills become the consiglieri for all others wishing to learn how to game the US welfare system.

If illegal aliens came to America seeking a better life and then chose to work for it and never took the amounts needed to support their lives in America, some Americans would say that was OK— even though their residency came about by them committing a crime. But, they learn early all about how to outfox a bunch of bureaucrats who might as well be wearing signs that say, "outfox me!" and the interlopers go ahead and outfox them.

These big mooches, whoever they are, need to be extricated from our country as soon as possible. We simply cannot afford them. We never could. We are $21 Trillion in debt trying to help the world while our own people are without jobs. We need to help ourselves first. The costs for interloper largesse is unsustainable as you will learn in this book.

This book announces a new program for America that Congress has not yet approved or considered. It is designed to help Americans and interlopers. It is built for Americans-first. However, it is also built to help interlopers escape the yoke of US managers who have them working for slave wages. This program can change their lives for the good, in ways they had never imagined.

I wrote this book to help Americans know what our President and Congress can do to force our government to regain control of our borders, ensure our national security, keep our culture, enforce our laws, protect American jobs, make our language the language of the nation, and keep all Americans from being overwhelmed by illegal foreign nationals who offer few benefits and no allegiance to America.

In addition to showing why amnesty is not the right medicine, I take the time to explain in detail the best plan for America to again become a sovereign state with America-loving Americans in charge.

You are going to love this book as well as the Pay-to-Go plan itself. With this plan, all interlopers will have the opportunity for a great life in their home countries with their complete families.

Illegal foreign nationals should be well pleased because the plan uses deportation as a very last resort and it immediately gets illegal foreign nationals out of the shadows as they await to return home. Few books are a must-read but Pay-to-Go: America-First Immigration Fix will quickly appear at the top of America's most read list. It also has a catchy subtitle. One of the big advantages for good-hearted Americans who are afraid of the pain that coerced deportations might cause the families of interlopers:

No More Deportations from America!!!

Table of Contents

Ch 1 Introduction to Pay-to-Go
A Land of Immigrants

The US for all of its existence, even before the War of Independence, would be characterized as a migrant receiving country. From colonial days until now our population went from a few thousand to 325 million and of course everybody here today was not born in America. We are truly a land of immigrants.

We currently take in a million to two million legal immigrants per year and from two-million to four million illegal immigrants aka foreign interlopers. The interlopers (uninvited "guests") get here by either crossing our borders without authorization or over staying legal visas. The four million figure comes from Senator John McCain, a well-known authority on immigration. The US is clearly the largest receiver of migrants in the world.

More and more Americans are finding it difficult to make ends meet in the new "COME ON DOWN" mentality fostered by government officials. The atmosphere today in America regarding the border interlopers, makes it seem like we have permanently positioned Bob Barker at the Border with a big megaphone: "Come on Down!"

Bobbarker

We'll take anybody today in the US, or so it seems. Nobody is checking. On the legal side, we even have a Visa Lottery because visas are so hard to get. 50,000 lucky people from across the world get to come to America for a life supported by American taxpayers.

You are in! You do not have to speak English and in fact, you don't have to speak at all. Say thanks to our corrupt Congress and our greedy businessmen for the lack of rules to protect American citizens.

If you resemble that remark, more than likely, you can thank past President Obama who continually intervened to assure nobody was left behind; nobody was really deported; and there were no restrictions on foreign interlopers taking American jobs—even those that had been in the family for years.

And, yes while simply being employed on a sub-minimum wage scale, our uninvited guests have unwittingly helped millions of greedy businesses lower their normal and customary wage in the country so that it is tough for anybody doing physical labor to make ends meet today.

The US has never used a pay-to-go approach in our history, but it is about time we gave it a try. Our treasury is being overwhelmed by demands from foreigners for more welfare. The cost of interlopers to our economy and our treasury is overwhelming.

Pay-to Go (receiving return transportation costs and a stipend for returning home from a host country such as the US) can even the playing field again and save the US hundreds of billions of dollars to boot.

Unlike America, other immigrant-receiving countries have for decades employed policies to encourage unauthorized immigrants to return to their home countries without the cost, legal barriers, and political obstacles of removals or forced returns—i.e. deportations. The US is a young country and we need to examine closely how others have dealt with excessive immigration and what can be termed pay to stay welfare benefits.

In other countries, nudging an interloper to go back home are a series of noncoercive, pay-to-go, voluntary, assisted voluntary, and non-forced returns. The countries generally offer paid travel and/or other financial incentives such as stipends to encourage unauthorized immigrants to cooperate with immigration officials and leave host countries to return home.

Ch 2 Pay-to-Go Plans in Other Countries
Paying a migrant to return home can work

Time Magazine online tells a story of Nexar Sambrano, who seemed to be living the immigrant dream in Spain. He had come to Barcelona in 2005 after leaving a near-subsistence existence on a farm in Ecuador. Times were good. He found a good-paying delivery job with the local beer company. Unfortunately, things changed.

After 18 months Nexar was doing so well and had tucked enough savings aside that he was hoping to bring his children and his girlfriend over to join him. Out of nowhere, the recession hit, and it affected everybody. Nexar lost his job. He was talented in the trades and was able to get by with odd jobs such a painting or doing masonry. However, it just was not enough.

Time quotes him as saying: "I was relying on my friends for food." So, when the Spanish government offered him money to go home, he took it.

When this Time piece was written it had been over two years since Spain had enacted its Voluntary Return Plan for immigrants, which grants legal residents who lose their jobs the right to receive their entire unemployment benefit in two lump sums — one upon departure, and the second after arriving in their country of origin. This is part of a trend in countries who had once been welcome hosts to migrants when things were good, and they needed extra labor to get the work done.

Over the last several years, some 17,000 documented migrants from the U.S., Eastern Europe, and Africa have signed on to the plan, part of a successful effort, says the government, to reduce the pressure on the Spanish economy and spark development in other parts of the world.

Too many people in a country is not good

The last thing that any country needs, especially as we have yet to fully climb out of The Great Recession is an excess of people. Among other things, they will be demanding to eat and to have a minimum of modest amenities. In the US of course, do-gooders want them all to have colored TV sets, iPads, and other goodies to make their stays comfortable. All of this is very costly to the host country.

Ch 3 Pay-to-Go Programs in History
The US would not be the first Pay-to-Go!

World governments have used voluntary return programs with stipend incentives (Pay-to-Go), and without incentives, long before the recent economic downturn and long before interlopers crossed borders illegally to take advantage of the host country's major benefit packages. Pay-to-Go has served various policy goals beyond coping with economic issues, such as what we are examining in America -- combating illegal immigration, addressing the detention of rejected asylum seekers, migrant over-population reduction, and promoting development through return migration.

For example, France, Germany, Belgium, and the Netherlands experimented with Pay-to-Go programs from the mid-1970s until the mid-1980s due to a poor economic climate, and the infamous 1973-1974 big oil embargo, among other circumstances. These countries sought to provide incentives for both employed and unemployed guest workers to return to their countries of origin. The host countries could not afford to keep them when their own people were not working.

Sixty million illegal foreign interlopers in the US today in a busted economy would not make the situation easier but for sure there would be a lot of takers.

The 2008-2009 Great Recession prompted massive unemployment among the approximately 350,000 Nikkeijin (Latin American workers residing in Japan who at one time emigrated from Japan), residing in Japan. Between November 2008 and January 2009, 9,296 foreigners registered as employment seekers. This was an 11-fold increase from the same period a year earlier.

There have been a number of immigration surveys conducted in Japan. Approximately 40 percent of Latin American workers, most of them Nikkeijin, were unemployed by the end of 2008 and the beginning of 2009, compared to the 5 percent unemployment rate among Brazilians and Peruvians in Japan in 2005.

The recession hit Nikkei (Nikkeijin) workers hardest, as many relied on contract-based employment and jobs that are sensitive to economic fluctuations.

With the economic hardships, massive return migration to Latin America has occurred, primarily due to large-scale layoffs of Nikkei workers and their inability to find new jobs before their unemployment insurance expires.

The point of all this discussion is that Japan uses incentive methods as necessary to move segments of the population to other countries to help its own citizens.

Ch 4 Pay-to-Go Down Under
No coercion necessary

The informal notion of a voluntary return or voluntary repatriation is most simply explained as a migrant, after arriving in a host state willingly deciding (no coercion) that they would like to return home (aka country of origin). More formally, we can say that it is the return of a displaced person, a rejected asylum seeker, a refugee, a victim of trafficking, or a stranded migrant who is unable or unwilling to remain in the host country and who volunteers to return to their country of origin.

There are various programs in different countries to help such people leave and return to their home countries when it is appropriate or simply when they are ready to come back home. The programs are most often built with some level of assistance in the expenses of travel to get home and sometimes they also include a stipend and sometimes they include assistance in the home country for reintegration and resettlement.

In Australia, for example, their AVR program is used as a vehicle to help migrants. It is also used to thin out any overpopulation of migrants who, in times of recession, may very well hold positions that citizens desire. The program helps the return of migrants who have no ongoing legal avenue to stay. However, the program once in effect is generally available to any migrant who needs assistance to return home.

Through small policy changes, Australia had been able to learn from AVR programs in other countries who are suffering similar circumstances with an over population of foreign-born non-citizens. The learning has helped Australia achieve a greater number of returns, thereby reducing the drain on their treasury.

As much as the US is a major magnet for the world's migrants, it is also substantially easier and far less expensive to get to than Australia. Australia might in fact be even more crowded than the US if the migrant population could get there by walking, by motor car or motor coach, or by railroad.

Pay-to-Go AVR programs

All AVR programs are designed to assist migrants to return home. The kind of assistance to a migrant varies from case to case depending on the national policy of a particular host country. The US would do well to follow Australia's lead.

I wrote this book to help Americans know what our President and Congress can do to help force our government to regain control of our borders, ensure our national security, keep our culture, enforce our laws, protect American jobs, make our language the language of the nation, and keep all Americans from being overwhelmed by illegal foreign nationals who offer few benefits and no allegiance to America.

Additionally, it is necessary for illegal foreign nationals to also be very pleased with a solution to their being stranded in our country living in poverty in our shadows. They should be happy with this plan which uses deportation as a very last resort and it immediately gets illegal foreign nationals out of the shadows and onto an all-expenses-paid trip back to their home country with a big wad of sheckles left for pocket change purchases and funding for a great start in their home country.

Chapter 11 60-Million Illegal Aliens in America!!!

60 MILLION
ILLEGAL ALIENS
IN AMERICA!!!
A simple, America-
first solution

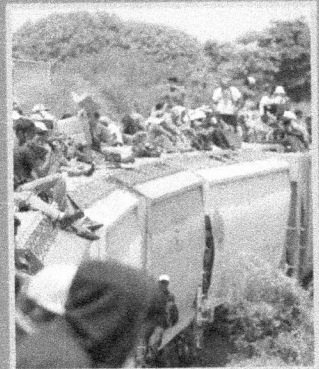

Brian W. Kelly

A simple, America-first solution.

Book purpose:

This book is a 2017 predecessor to books already examined titled, *Pay to Go* and *Legalizing Illegal Aliens via Resident Visas*. In this book, the **Pay-to-Go Plan** as originally conceived was called **The Stipend Return Plan.** It was just about the same as *Pay-to-Go. In* conjunction with the *Resident Visa*, the total plan revealed first in this book, solves the problem of 60 million illegal interlopers resident in America. This book has more details than the other two.

Donald Trump is on America's side

Donald Trump's signature issue from the announcement of his presidential candidacy has been immigration reform because he loves America and Americans. Trump of course has been focused in preventing entry for intruders by building a big beautiful wall, whereas this book deals head-on with the problem of 60 million resident illegal aliens. Both notions should be part of the administration's immigration strategy.

As difficult as it is for good, hard-working Americans to believe, our government has been working to keep us poor. Former President Obama's de-facto amnesties and a do-nothing Congress made it tough for Americans to find work while competing against foreign interlopers whose minimal wage demands gave them the advantage in the jobs marketplace.

Congress has been laying low and lying when necessary. Unfortunately, their efforts have produced a terrible truth— Americans have been left behind and nobody cares. Meanwhile, uninvited guests, working for peanuts, have reduced wages and taken the few jobs that exist today. After they get here, these poor souls languish in misery and a lifetime of poverty as even what they take from our welfare system is hardly enough to keep them going.

Reviewers of this two-part plan can see that the Resident Visa Plan will help Americans first and that it is also designed to help illegal foreign nationals in have a better life also. They will no longer be chained to greedy businesses looking for slave-labor wages.

The Resident Visa Plan takes interlopers out of the shadows and gives them opportunity. If well-behaved, they gain the right to stay and work in America for a lifetime, one year at a time. They will be out of the shadows with no amnesty, no citizenship, no freebies, no line jumping; and no jobs before Americans. The Stipend-Return Plan will provide a nice dollar bonus to any illegal alien that wants a free trip home with money in their pocket. In a subsequent book, shown previously, we call this Pay-to-Go.

These US immigration goals are satisfied in the Resident Visa Plan and for those who would rather a jump start back in their home country, the Stipend Return plan puts money in their pockets as soon as they arrive in their home country. These two plans are destined to save America a half-Trillion dollars each year.

Those who sign up for the program that permits them to stay in America, must be vetted every year and must pay a fee each year or be deported. There's lots more! You're going to like this America-first plan built by an American for Americans.

Preface:

What would you call a plan that solved a problem for America that most of the Congress seems to have no interest in solving? I have called it many things while perfecting this book, but now let me settle with what I would like to call **The Stipend Return / Resident Visa Plan**.

I had called the plan many things but never hit the nail on the head. This is my vision for a secret sauce solution to fix the problem of 60 million interlopers waking up in America every day. Yes—build the wall, please! But simultaneously solve the residence problem of so many people who do not belong here. Do we really need up to 60 million interlopers in residence? I do not think so. Hey, John McCain thinks there are over 128 million interlopers in residence.

There are many problems with illegal immigration. For the United States, the biggest problem is the fact that the cost of welfare, cash payments, and medical assistance is bankrupting the country. We cannot afford the huge cost that illegal interlopers place on our system when most of them, because of their reliance on identity theft and mad-up fake ID's, collect some form of welfare.

Every resident feels about a $1500 burden from the generous plans that help illegal residents survive in America's shadows. Additionally, wages for Americans are always going down while expenses are going up. The new Stipend Return / Resident Visa program solves both of these problems at the same time.

I am happy that you are reading this book and I hope many others find it and convince the Administration and the Congress and the President that it is their turn to learn about The Resident Visa Plan.

This book is the result of over ten years of work from way back when I wrote my first patriotic book in 2006 titled Taxation without Representation. The 4th edition is now current. The Resident Visa Plan was formalized in 2013 under a different title.

At the time that this work evolved to its current shape, I had examined everything out there especially the Gang of Eight Plan (GO8), existing law, and other notions about how anybody might possibly solve the nation's concerns about 60 million illegal residents.

At first look, I found no real solutions other than either amnesty or follow the law with deportation. The Resident Visa solution is unique, and everything needed to implement it is already in place.

The Resident Visa solution directly addresses the issues that having 60 million illegal foreign nationals in residence have brought upon America. The Gang of Eight approach rewards illegal activity and makes everybody OK and is a bad example, and another approach gives most people a bad, sinking feeling in their gut. That's why nobody has come forward to suggest that 100% deportations are really a good idea for the country. Americans have big hearts.

Deportation is fair of course as these folks have broken our laws. But, our politicians are culpable as they made it too easy for foreigners to break our laws. Amnesty is not a solution as Americans have already paid a big price for the largesse of politicians wanting low wages and those wanting the future votes of today's interlopers.

Ideally, the solution would be to go poof, and every foreign interloper would be taken back to where and when they crossed the border years and years ago. Where is a used Star-Trek Transporter when we need one? This time, however, they would not be re-admitted if they tried to cross.

The raw facts say that the problem never should have reached the level of severity that it is today. Nobody can perform miracles and tricorders and transporters are not invented yet so when we have the closest ingenious thought to a miracle as a solution, we should examine it and embrace it. It is this plan. Doing nothing makes it worse.

After defining the problem in my early books, I developed a methodology that would make Americans pleased and would remove all interlopers from the shadows—and into the light of the American day or back home with some cash in their pockets if they choose.

Americans in this system would have priority and for their right to participate, interlopers would agree to pay their own way while in our country. Such a plan ought to work. Only the bad guys would be deported.

When I carefully read the Gang of Eight "comprehensive" plan in 2013, I noticed that it smelled a lot like it was purposely designed to kill America. No jobs would be left for Americans. Newly unemployed Americans would have to pay for newly minted citizens getting a lifetime of freebies. We would see them voting in national elections; and watch their numbers grow until there were 33 million more foreign nationals looking for jobs by plan—jobs that Americans cannot even find.

Per Heritage.org, the cost for the 33 million that were intended to be brought in by reunification provisions of the Gang of 8 Bill, was estimated at well over $6 Trillion. Even Donald Trump does not have that much money. I think. The bottom line is that this was a terrible deal for the country.

I was hunting for a real immigration fix that pleased Americans. Marco Rubio, Chuck Schumer and the rest of the Gang of Eight were looking for scalps to prove to Democrats that they had the progressive agenda in the forefront. Let me tell you now folks. I do not. Like they did in the 1920's, progressives are again trying to undermine America.

I looked at all the things that Americans want in a real plan— things they liked and things they do not like. I wanted interlopers to embrace the plan, so they could get out of the shadows without hurting Americans. So, among other things, I examined what interlopers liked about living in America.

In my first cut at solving the problem in 2013, I figured out a way to permit well-behaved interlopers to stay in America one year at a time with a realistic annual renewal fee, while giving Americans priority in all ways. It was a good plan but not as perfect as I had hoped. The biggest problem with the plan was that it was difficult to explain in clear concise terms.

I was convinced that the plan actually would work and that it would solve the problem for the long haul and take a huge financial burden off the backs of Americans. And, so, I kept at it, continually improving it until it was perfected.

Every plan requires fine tuning and we would expect this to continue to be the case with the Resident Visa Plan. By implementing the current iteration of the plan, the long-sought solution to the result of illegal immigration is around the corner.

To see what US officials on the pro-American side of the issue would think about such a plan for America, I contacted Pennsylvania Congressman, Lou Barletta. Many know Lou Barletta as a tireless advocate for fighting illegal immigration and amnesty. He is running for the Senate against a very poor legislator, Bob Casey, Jr., in my state of Pennsylvania. I presented a detailed PowerPoint of my ideas in late January 2015 to the Congressman and his chief aid at the time, Joseph Gerdes. After perfecting the plan even more, I reached out again and presented again in 2016 to the Congressman. I am scheduled for another meeting soon.

The Congressman was most pleased with my presentation and the detail that backed up each and every point of the presentation. The Congressman and I continued to engage in a lengthy dialogue on these issues. We spoke about the difficulties in getting immigration legislation for Americans through the House and the Senate, and he updated me as to where the Congress was with some new initiatives in securing the border.

During this interchange, the Congressman helped me understand what was really happening in Washington. For my part, I helped the Congressman to fully understand the benefits of this immigration fix for as many as 60 million foreign nationals residing illegally in America.

Both Congressman Barletta and President Trump have made the wall and border security their # 1 priorities. This plan addresses those interlopers who are already here. We need to protect the border and handle the 60 million interlopers at the same time for the good of America.

My strong recommendation to Congressman Barletta and President Trump is that we add this immigration fix, which I call "The Resident Visa Plan," to the "Beautiful Wall" and the Bills and the Amendments on Border Security. This would be the best anybody could do to solve the problem of resident interlopers in America once and for all.

This would be the first comprehensive and comprehensible immigration plan ever put forward that favored America and Americans over foreign nationals. It is America-First.

I sent the Congressman a text version of the presentation with its new logical flow so that he could take it, read it, and share it without having to figure out the hidden messages within the bullets of a PowerPoint. This new update and the updates in the two books subsequent to this will be in Senator Barletta's hands at the same time that they are on the street for sale.

As I examined the document that I produced that comprises this book, I realized that it was much more complete than the original

Kelly Plan. Its sequencing is much better; and the additions from the Barletta presentation / interview add a lot of missing pieces to the package. And, so, I decided to re-work the text document to make it even better.

In 2013, Americans rejected the Gang of Eight Amnesty Bill. So, here I am again, in my 129th book writing again about the problem of 60 million interlopers making it tough for Americans. This time, however, it is far more simplified and easier to implement.

A key element of this plan is that each year the clock resets on foreign nationals who are permitted here under the Resident Visa Plan. This book, thus focuses on interlopers signing up to become Resident Visa Holders with appropriate renewal assurances for good behavior.

This is **the** tool to accomplish the goal of an America and American-First solution to 60 million interlopers. There are a lot of other adjunct notions besides the Resident Visa Plan such as a solution for visa over stayers, green card holders, as well as a unique solution for current birthright citizens.

The solution for the illegal interloper issue is large enough to warrant its own book. President Trump already has a team of people working on other solutions in the immigration umbrella such as border security and the wall, visa overstays, sanctuary cities and other issues not directly related to the 60 million interlopers taking from Americans every day.

You won't believe how easy the problem of 60 million interlopers is to solve if we can get our legislators to take action or President Trump finds he can take Executive Action.

In summary, this book presents the Resident Visa Plan as the fix and the Stipend Return Plan as a backup fix. Then it offers many other points on why this is the one and only fix to create an America without shadows that favors Americans 100%. There is so much good left over that good-willed interlopers have a lot to gain simply by signing up.

I wrote this book to help Americans know what our President and Congress can do to force our government to regain control of our borders, ensure our national security, keep our culture, enforce our laws, protect American jobs, make our language the language of the nation, and keep all Americans from being overwhelmed by illegal foreign nationals who offer few benefits and no allegiance to America.

In addition to showing why amnesty is not the right medicine, I take the time to explain in detail the best plan for America to again become a sovereign state with America-loving Americans in charge.

You are going to love this book as well as the plan itself. All interlopers immediately are to be registered and accountable. You will see that The Resident Visa Plan (SR/RV) is designed by an American for Americans.

Additionally, illegal foreign nationals will be very pleased because the plan uses deportation as a very last resort and it immediately gets illegal foreign nationals out of the shadows. Few books are a must-read but 60 Million Illegal Aliens in America Is a Big Problem will quickly appear at the top of America's most read list. It also has a catchy subtitle:

This is a simple, America-first solution if Congress and the President have the guts! It solves the problem!

Table of Contents

Ch 1 The CliffsNotes Version
60 million interlopers in 60 seconds

I do not have to go far out on a limb to suggest that if we knew how to immediately stop the drain on our government treasuries with one bold and very fair move, our representatives would be forced to adopt the measures necessary to achieve the gains. In this case, it would be to stop the major treasury drain that occurs each and every day to support a population segment of illegal interlopers. The term interloper, whether legal or illegal, means *uninvited guest*.

Based on what it costs to support illegal foreign nationals. we can certainly afford to deport millions of people. However, there are many good reasons why we should not deport anybody other than criminals. Most of the 60 million illegal residents are hardworking and living quiet, orderly lives. We also cannot allow them, as a result of their illegal entry, to become citizens. This would violate the basic premise of following the rule of law that is a key standard of citizenship. This book offers two great solutions to solve this big problem.

By the way, in this abbreviated "CliffsNotes" chapter, we net it out, so it can be well understood. I predict that the biggest obstacle in solving the problem of 60 million illegal interlopers in America will be both chambers of the US Congress. I am not naïve enough to suggest that the current Congress' predilection for more voters and lower wages for all Americans could be overcome by the fact that this plan to deal with resident interlopers is the best yet conceived. So, we may be forced to replace them all (Congress) in order to do the right thing for America.

We cannot let our corrupt Congress get in the way of our solving our problem with the 60 million. I admit that this would probably be more difficult than stopping the treasury loss but at least we would all know what we must do, and seeing Congress packing would be a pleasure to the senses.

John McCain is known for his estimate of a clip of about 4 million per year. Illegal aliens (interlopers) have chosen to cross the southern border or they have chosen to simply overstay their visas in order to gain residence in the US. Amnesty advocate John McCain, who is a recognized authority on the subject of illegal immigration, in a letter dated February 2004, wrote that apprehension figures demonstrated that "almost four million people crossed the US border illegally in 2002."

McCain estimates over 10,000 cross every day. Adding it up, that comes to 128 million by the end of 2017. If we cut that in half and round it down, we're looking at my estimate of 60 million interlopers in residence today. I know that nobody can prove me wrong.

The name of the plan to solve the problem of 60 million interlopers makes sense when you think about it. It is the *Stipend Return / Resident Visa Plan*. The little slash means *or* in this case. The program immediately takes 60 million illegal foreign nationals out of the shadows and saves the US treasury a minimum of a half-Trillion dollars each year after year 1. Should Congress and /or the President pursue this plan? Of course!

What problem does the program fix? It is a pro-America and pro-American citizen solution. It is an America-First solution to the major problem of 60 million illegal residents sponging off the taxpayers in the United States. Once in the continental US, the interlopers either wholly or partially depend on US taxpayer dollars for their daily sustenance. Is your wallet looking a little thinner these days? The problem we plan to solve in this book, *the real problem,* is that 60 million illegal foreign nationals cost Americans money every day. They just don't pay their way and live here. They take from US.

...

What if interlopers do not want to go home

If a resident illegal foreign national really does not want to go home regardless of the incentive, then there is another option that actually costs taxpayers nothing and permits the interloper to stay in America indefinitely in a legal state as long as they "behave." The program provides for granting interlopers in good standing what we are about to call a Resident Visa. This is a new visa type that, unlike other visa types can be renewed each and every year with conditions.

With this, former foreign nationals would be legal under the protection of the Resident Visa and could remain in America as long as they behave in a lawful manner according to the exact terms of their visa.

There are many differences between illegally gaining benefits in the United States and becoming legal by gaining a Resident Visa. Those choosing to employ the Resident Visa to stay in America, are welcome to do so; but the terms of the relationship with US officials will not be the same as when they were illegal.

For example, there would be no more cash incentives. The former interloper would be temporarily legalized after applying for a special US passport and then a Resident Visa and after being approved for both. The visa will be special in that it will be renewable with a fee of $100 required annually after a renewal application, a record update (demographics, etc.), and a re-vetting of the applicant, and a special oath of allegiance.

Why should an illegal alien residing in America in the shadows find either of these two different plans acceptable?

- ✓ Stipend-Assisted Return Program
- ✓ Resident Visa Program

1. No more living in the shadows of America.
2. Opportunity to go home travel-free if desired with a big stipend paid by Americans.
3. US will budget $15 Billion for safe cities in home countries for returning immigrants
4. US will develop 15 safe settlements / cities with 10 in Mexico
5. Can get in line (back of line) in home country for citizenship without leaving US.
6. With renewals, the opportunity to live in America a lifetime.
7. Can obtain a driver's license, insurance, etc.
8. Can keep any job that is already held.
9. Can apply for any job available in America.

10. Can live wherever they want in America.
11. Can get same paid by patient medical insurance as Americans.
12. Can get installment loans from US Government on an exception basis to help with medical and educational expenses. Must be paid back.
13. After five years but no more, living with a Resident Visa, can still opt for stipend to go home.
14. Anchor family stipends to go home are huge ($50,000 per birthright citizen) and cumulative with a no-return promise.

I would suspect that list above provides a lot more advantages for interlopers than most would ever believe from how the corrupt US press will preview this program. Yet, this is just one of two major options that under the Stipend Return / Resident Visa Program, from which illegal residents may choose.

Many of the advantages for current interlopers are listed in the fourteen points above. The first plan provides a pay-to-go option that is more generous than any other country in the world. The second plan is the Resident Visa Program since getting a Resident Visa is all that is needed to win the illegal alien game. If you want to win and stay in America, this is the plan for you.

Winning the illegal alien game thankfully does not mean that Americans are shut out. Any illegal foreign national who opts for the stipend deal and departs for home under the Stipend-Assisted Return Program should have no regrets as all expenses are paid and the stipend is nice, and it includes $20,000 for each alien dependent who are also in the program. A three-child family can provide a $100,000 stipend for the family in the home country and the US can more than afford to pay it.

Knowing this is so beneficial to interlopers, why should Joe America want this program? In a nutshell, it is because Joe America is smart and knows this will save a ton of dollars for him and all Americans.

Many Americans do not trust the government, period. So, why would Americans think this is a good deal if the illegal foreign national does not choose to exit America with a stipend? Then what?

If an illegal foreign national chooses not to accept this US government act of kindness, and does not go home, and does not sign up for The Resident Visa Program—the only two options in the Stipend Return / Resident Visa Program, there is only one course of action left for the government. The interloper will be asked to leave the country at their own expense. They will be deported otherwise.

By the enactment of this new visa and this new "return home" plan, the idea of residing in America in an illegal alien status is being eliminated, period. The lack of a decision by an illegal interloper to choose one or the other will unfortunately provoke immigration authorities to deport them.

Why should an American citizen like these two plans?

1. The days of the free lunch are over.
2. Fee based passport & Resident Visa is designed to be cost free to Americans
3. Return Home stipends pay for themselves in one year
4. Illegal aliens must agree to terms of Resident Visa-- all benefits eliminated after 1st year.
5. Once an illegal alien returns home, cannot come back; no cost is accrued after year 1
6. No birthright citizenship for illegals, permanent residents, and Resident Visa Holders
7. No cash, medical services, education, welfare, or other benefits permitted for those with a Resident Visa.
8. No citizen-only privileges permitted
9. Resident Visa Holders have no right to vote in any election
10. New jobs must go to American citizens first—all things being equal.
11. Fees, fines on employers will help pay for Resident Visa program kickoff. Will generate approximately $400 Billion.
12. When program in high gear, US will save more than $500 Billion per year on interloper expenses.
13. Resident Visa holder must be employed (1 yr. to get a job)
14. Resident Visa holder must have self-paid or employer-paid healthcare
15. Resident Visa holder must pass English test in two years

16. Resident Visa holder must take oath of allegiance to be approved for 1st renewal
17. No more green cards for family reunification-instead use Resident Visa.
18. All green card permanent residence visas are eliminated when expired. No new green cards. Use Resident Visa.
19. Next 10-yr green card renewal becomes a Resident Visa
20. No path to citizenship without going home to get in line (begin a process like all others from that country)
21. Citizenship line -- jumping the line is not permitted.
22. Major cost savings for America

The end of Sanctuary Cities

Victor David Hanson writes: "Sanctuary cities protect illegal aliens from federal immigration agencies in a way that is not true of American citizens who arrive at airports and must go through customs, with no exemption from federal agents examining their passports and personal histories. If crimes or infractions are found, there is no safe space at an airport exempt from federal enforcement."

The SR/RV program either pays illegal interlopers to go or it provides a Resident Visa that offers many benefits to both interlopers and American citizens. For example, it saves about $500,000,000,000 per year after year one of its implementation. With no more illegal aliens in the country, a major advantage is that the divisive notion of Sanctuary Cities and the term Sanctuary Cities can be removed from the US vocabulary. There will be no need for them with residents all being legal.

Anchor babies qualify

The Stipend Return program is also available to those who became citizens through the anchor baby loophole of the 14th amendment. When an Anchor child with parent chooses to join the Stipend Return program, each anchor citizen child will receive a $50,000 stipend and each of his or her interloper parents will receive their own $20,000 for a total of $70,000 for a two-person family and $90,000 for a three-person family with one child. A family of four anchor children with a mom or dad would receive $240,000. With mom and dad, the sum would be $240,000. This is very affordable for US citizens considering the lifetime cost of one anchor baby can be as much as $2 million or more.

DACA "children" also qualify

The SRRV program solves the problem for DACA children also. DACA children qualify for the full $20,000 stipend in the Stipend Return Program. Those in the DACA program also qualify for the Resident Visa Program if they want to stay in the US. As an additional DACA concession for the "Children" who opt for the Resident Visa, there will be no charge for the visa for the first five renewal years. DACA "children" will be vetted when they apply for a resident passport. Gang members, of course, will be deported without benefits.

The evidence is on the table.

Nobody in their right mind wants life to continue with a shadow population who in many ways have been victimized similar to how slaves were victimized many years ago. The Stipend Return and the Resident Visa are programs that provide a way out of the mess for both interlopers and regular Americans.

Greedy fat cat business persons and politicians at the highest levels created this mess for both factions. Consequently, the plan includes substantial fees and fines for those businesses who hired illegal interlopers instead of Americans. Being greedy will cost the fat cats over $400 Billion and perhaps more.

They made a ton of money off the backs of Americans with lower wages while poor interlopers were living in squalor with sub-minimum wages. American industry as represented by the Chamber of Commerce should show some remorse and voluntarily chip in to help solve this problem and back the Stipend Return / Residence Visa Plan as it is a winner for all decent Americans and the long-suffering communities whose only solace is the shadows of America.

Quick Comparison with the Gang of Eight

In 2013, eight US Senators known as the Gang of Eight got a bill passed in the Senate that sold Americans down the river and would have given a ton of benefits to illegal aliens at taxpayer cost. The Stipend Return / Resident Visa Program is pro-American and saves taxpayers substantial dollars. It is nothing like the John McCain / Marco Rubio Gof8 sellout. It is explained in detail later in the book. For now, the following quick comparison chart is shown to help us better understand the new combined program by comparing it in the chart below with the Gang of Eight Program

2013 Gang of Eight v Resident Visa

	G of 8	SR/RV
Border secure	No	More technology
Jobs	Favors Interlopers	Favors Americans
Amnesty	Yes	No
Path to citizenship	Yes	No (almost same as today)
Permanent residents	Yes	Never, renewable visa
Voting	Yes	No, Never
Welfare benefits	Yes	No, Never
Freebies	Yes	No, Never
Anchor babies	Yes	No, stipends to depart
Employer fees/fines	No	Yes -if one illegal employee
Reunification	33M in 10yrs	Not Resident Visa Holders
Coerced-deportation	None	As needed for violations
Return to home country	No	Yes, with stipend
Must have healthcare	No	Yes
Must be employed	No	Yes
Must speak English in 2 yrs?	No	Yes
Oath of allegiance	No	Yes, after 1 year
Cost/debt accountability	No	Yes
Taxpayer Costs	$ 6Trillion	Zero
Payback plan	No	Yes
Accountability Database	No	Yes
Interloper fine	Yes	Yes
Employer fine	No	Yes (helps finance program)
Back taxes	No	Yes (vetting interviews)

Other books by Brian Kelly: (amazon.com, and Kindle)

Boost Social Security Now! Hey Buddy Can You Spare a Dime?
The Birth of American Football. From the first college game in 1869 to the last Super Bowl
Obamacare: A One-Line Repeal Congress must get this done.
A Wilkes-Barre Christmas Story A wonderful town makes Christmas all the better
A Boy, A Bike, A Train, and a Christmas Miracle A Christmas story that will melt your heart
Pay-to-Go   America-First Immigration Fix
Legalizing Illegal Aliens Via Resident Visas Americans-first plan saves $Trillions. Learn how!
60 Million Illegal Aliens in America!!! A simple, America-first solution.
The Bill of Rights By Founder James Madison Refresh your knowledge of the specific rights for all
Great Players in Army Football Great Army Football played by great players..
Great Coaches in Army Football Army's coaches are all great.
Great Moments in Army Football Army Football at its best.
Great Moments in Florida Gators Football Gators Football from the start. This is the book.
Great Moments in Clemson Football CU Football at its best. This is the book.
Great Moments in Florida Gators Football Gators Football from the start. This is the book.
The Constitution Companion. A Guide to Reading and Comprehending the Constitution
The Constitution by Hamilton, Jefferson, & Madison – Big type and in English
PATERNO: The Dark Days After Win # 409. Sky began to fall within days of win # 409.
JoePa 409 Victories: Say No More! Winningest Division I-A football coach ever
American College Football: The Beginning From before day one football was played.
Great Coaches in Alabama Football Challenging the coaches of every other program!
Great Coaches in Penn State Football the Best Coaches in PSU's football program
Great Players in Penn State Football The best players in PSU's football program
Great Players in Notre Dame Football The best players in ND's football program
Great Coaches in Notre Dame Football The best coaches in any football program
Great Players in Alabama Football from Quarterbacks to offensive Linemen Greats!
Great Moments in Alabama Football AU Football from the start. This is the book.
Great Moments in Penn State Football PSU Football, start--games, coaches, players,
Great Moments in Notre Dame Football ND Football, start, games, coaches, players
Cross Country With the Parents A great trip from East Coast to West with the kids
Seniors, Social Security & the Minimum Wage. Things seniors need to know.
How to Write Your First Book and Publish It with CreateSpace
The US Immigration Fix--It's all in here. Finally, an answer.
I had a Dream IBM Could be #1 Again The title is self-explanatory
WineDiets.Com Presents The Wine Diet Learn how to lose weight while having fun.
Wilkes-Barre, PA; Return to Glory Wilkes-Barre City's return to glory
Geoffrey Parsons' Epoch... The Land of Fair Play Better than the original.
The Bill of Rights 4 Dummmies! This is the best book to learn about your rights.
Sol Bloom's Epoch ...Story of the Constitution The best book to learn the Constitution
America 4 Dummmies! All Americans should read to learn about this great country.
The Electoral College 4 Dummmies! How does it really work?
The All-Everything Machine Story about IBM's finest computer server.
ThankYou IBM! This book explains how IBM was beaten in the computer marketplace by neophytes

Brian has written 146 books in total. Other books can be found at amazon.com/author/brianwkelly

www.ingramcontent.com/pod-product-compliance
Lightning Source LLC
Chambersburg PA
CBHW070934280326
41934CB00009B/1868